# Cairn Terrier

## Hero of Oz

### by Duncan Searl

Consultants:

John Cleland
President of the Potomac Cairn
Terrier Club (2005–2010)

Lois Cleland
Co-Rescue Chairperson of the
Potomac Cairn Terrier Club

**BEARPORT**
PUBLISHING

New York, New York

## Credits

Cover and Title Page, © Yann Arthus-Bertrand/Corbis; TOC, © Eric Isselée/Shutterstock; 4, © Moviestore Collection Ltd/Alamy; 5T, © Everett Collection, Inc; 5B, © Corbis; 6, © Christie's Images Ltd./SuperStock; 7, © Graham Uney/Alamy; 8, © Paris Pierce/Alamy; 9TL, © J. De Meester/Arco Images/Alamy; 9TR, © Jerry Shulman/SuperStock; 9BL, © Barbara Von Hoffmann/Animals Animals Enterprises; 9BR, © Olga Drozdova/iStockphoto; 10, © tbkmedia.de/Alamy; 11L, © Mary Bloom; 11R, © Mary Bloom; 12, © Farlap/Alamy; 13L, © Amir Paz/PhotoStock-Israel 13R, © Jeannie Harrison/Close Encounters of the Furry Kind; 14, © Debby Lajeunesse; 15L, © Debby Lajeunesse; 15R, © Debby Lajeunesse; 16T, © Harry Cornelius; 16B, Courtesy of Onesojourner; 17, © Jeannie Harrison/Close Encounters of the Furry Kind; 18, © David Hosking/FLPA/age fotostock; 19L, © Mary Bloom; 19R, © Visual&Written/Newscom; 20, © AP Images/Martin Cleaver; 21L, © Tristan Hawke/PhotoStockFile/Alamy; 21R, © A. Niehues/age fotostock; 22L, Courtesy of Ann Brodie, photo by Bob Gann; 22R, © Kathy Engel Stable; 23T, Courtesy of Fred Trzos; 23B, © Mike Bilbo; 24T, © MGM/The Kobal Collection/Picture-desk; 24B, © MGM/Photofest; 25, © Everett Collection, Inc; 26, © CBS/Photofest; 27, © Jeannie Harrison/Close Encounters of the Furry Kind; 28, © Petra Wegner/Alamy; 29T, © Eric Isselée/Shutterstock; 29B, © Dave King/Dorling Kindersley; 31, © Eric Isselée/Shutterstock; 32, © Lars Christensen/Shutterstock.

Publisher: Kenn Goin
Senior Editor: Lisa Wiseman
Creative Director: Spencer Brinker
Original Design: Dawn Beard Creative
Photo Researcher: Amy Dunleavy

*Library of Congress Cataloging-in-Publication Data*

Searl, Duncan.
  Cairn terrier : hero of Oz / by Duncan Searl.
    p. cm. — (Little dogs rock II)
  Includes bibliographical references and index.
  ISBN-13: 978-1-936088-16-4 (library binding)
  ISBN-10: 1-936088-16-9 (library binding)
  1. Cairn terrier—Juvenile literature. I. Title.
  SF429.C3S43 2011
  636.755—dc22
                    2010014025

For more information, write to Bearport Publishing Company, Inc., 101 Fifth Avenue, Suite 6R, New York, New York 10003. Printed in the United States of America in North Mankato, Minnesota.

072010
042110CGF

10 9 8 7 6 5 4 3 2 1

# Contents

# A Star

Poor Terry. Becoming a movie star wasn't easy. The little Cairn terrier had played only a few small parts in films. What she needed was a big role.

In 1938, Terry finally got her break. MGM Studios, a movie company, needed to fill a key role in a major new film. Studio officials wanted Terry to try out for the part.

Terry the Cairn terrier

Terry's manager, Carl Spitz, drove her to the audition. The studio officials took one look and hired her. The **scrappy** little dog was perfect for the part.

The new film was called *The Wizard of Oz*. Terry would be playing the role of Toto. Little did she know that she was about to become the most famous Cairn terrier of all time!

◀ A movie poster from the film *The Wizard of Oz*

Terry was a female Cairn terrier. However, in *The Wizard of Oz*, she played a male dog.

Dog trainer Carl ▶ Spitz rescued Terry from a dog shelter.

# Back in Time

The Highlands of Scotland are a long way from Hollywood, California, but that's where Terry's **ancestors** got their start. Life in the Highlands was hard in the 1700s. The climate was wet and cold, and the land was rocky. Farmers called **crofters** raised sheep and grew oats. However, there was never enough to eat.

**Crofters lived ▶ in homes such as this one.**

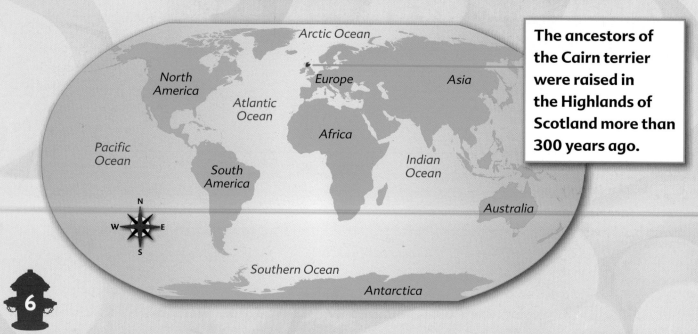

Arctic Ocean

North America

Europe

Asia

Atlantic Ocean

Africa

Pacific Ocean

South America

Indian Ocean

Australia

N
W E
S

Southern Ocean

Antarctica

**The ancestors of the Cairn terrier were raised in the Highlands of Scotland more than 300 years ago.**

To make matters worse, rats, weasels, and foxes often stole the crofters' food. These wild animals lived in cairns, or rock piles, that dotted the landscape. To survive, the crofters had to figure out a way to control these pests.

To solve this problem, they **bred** small fierce terriers that weighed about 15 pounds (6.8 kg). These brave dogs were the perfect size to squirm through the tiny openings in the cairns and catch their **prey**.

Terriers are a type of dog that love to dig. Their name comes from *terra*, the Latin word for "earth."

▲ Small animals, such as rats and mice, made their dens in cairns like this one.

# Four Breeds from One

The little terriers of the Highlands were **working dogs**. They were bred for their courage and ability to hunt, not for their looks.

In fact, the appearance of the dogs varied from area to area. Some had long hair and others had short hair. There were all-white terriers and there were some that came in other colors.

**The terriers of the Highlands came in many different colors.** ▶

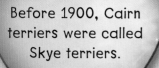
Before 1900, Cairn terriers were called Skye terriers.

During the 1800s, people began to keep these dogs as pets. Some preferred the long-haired dogs, while others liked the short-haired terriers. Still others preferred the all-white ones. By the early 1900s, the dogs were separated into four official **breeds**—the Scottish terrier, the West Highland white terrier, the Dandie Dinmont terrier, and the Cairn terrier.

▲ **Scottish terrier**

▲ **West Highland white terrier**

▲ **Dandie Dinmont terrier**

▲ **Cairn terrier**

# Colorful Coats

Just like their relatives, the Cairn terriers of today are a very colorful breed. They can be black, gray, red, **wheaten**—anything but white. The dogs can also be brindled. This means they are gray or tan and streaked with a darker color.

Whatever the dog's color, every Cairn terrier has two **coats**. The outer coat, called the topcoat, is coarse and helps keep the dog dry and clean. The **undercoat** is soft and furry and helps keep the terrier warm.

▲ **A dark brindle Cairn terrier (left),
a red brindle Cairn terrier (middle),
and a wheaten Cairn terrier (right)**

The color of a Cairn's coat often changes to another color as the dog ages.

To keep a Cairn's coat looking its best, **groomers** don't clip the dog's hair. Instead, they pull the old hair out by the roots. This doesn't hurt the dog, and it lets new hair grow in more easily.

◁ Cairns shed little to no hair, but they should be brushed weekly.

▲ A groomer pulling out a Cairn terrier's hair

# Today's High Standards

In the United States, the **American Kennel Club** (AKC) keeps records of all the different kinds of dog breeds and their **standards**, which describe the ideal appearance of each type of dog. At dog shows, judges use these standards to pick the **Best in Show**.

The ideal Cairn has a wide skull, a black nose, and a strong muzzle. Its hazel-colored eyes should be set wide apart, while its small, pointy ears should stand straight up.

What is the AKC standard for a Cairn terrier? As a small dog, it should weigh between 13 and 14 pounds (5.9 and 6.4 kg). Its height at the **withers** should be 9.5 to 10 inches (24.1 to 25.4 cm). From its chest to its **hindquarters**, a Cairn should measure 14.25 to 15 inches (36.2 to 38.1 cm) long.

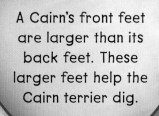

A Cairn's front feet are larger than its back feet. These larger feet help the Cairn terrier dig.

▲ **During a dog show, a Cairn should move actively with its tail held straight in the air.**

# A Visit to a Breeder

Cairn terrier standards are important to breeders like Debra Lajeunesse. She has bred prize-winning Cairns for more than 17 years. "The standards help me make breeding decisions," said Debra. "One of my females, for example, was slightly short. So I bred her with a tall male. The puppies met the standard perfectly!"

Like all breeders, Debra keeps records of each dog's **lineage**. Knowing about a dog's family is the best way to breed healthy, prize-winning puppies.

▲ **Debra with her Cairn terriers**

The age of the female is important, too. "I breed a female only two times," Debra explains, "first when she's two years old, and again when she's three. After that, she can rest."

Not that these **feisty** little dogs rest often. Molly, an 11-year-old Cairn that lives at Debra's **kennel**, is always in motion. If she's not going up and down the slide or jumping hurdles, then she is playfully chasing the puppies around.

◄ **Cairns love to play. Here, Cliffie enjoys the slide at Debra's kennel.**

Though they are small, Cairn terriers do need to exercise. It's important for owners to take their pets for a daily walk.

**Eleven-year-old Molly** ▶ **is Debra's oldest dog.**

# Puppy Love

Cairn terriers are little from the start. A newborn pup weighs about six ounces (170 g)—that's small enough for a person to hold in the palm of his or her hand.

Like most puppies, Cairn terriers cannot see or hear at birth. Their eyes and ears open after a week or two. At three weeks, they begin to walk. Given the chance, they'll even start to dig!

**A Cairn mother with her pups**

◄ **A nine-week-old Cairn pup**

Mother Cairn terriers have four to six puppies in one **litter**.

When Cairn terriers are 10 to 12 weeks old, they can leave their mothers. Adopting a Cairn puppy is a big decision. Not everyone has the time and energy it takes to raise one of these little dogs.

▲ **Cairns make lovable pets, but they are also a big responsibility.**

# A Mind of Its Own

Cairn terriers are popular pets, but they can be **assertive**. Given the chance, they might try to take over the families that adopt them. By barking often and jumping up on people, a Cairn is saying, "I'm in charge here!" It's up to the dog's owner to provide good training for his or her little pet.

▲ Cairn terrier owners must teach their pets not to jump on people.

Luckily, Cairns are smart and easy to train. They quickly learn to sit, **heel**, and lie down. While the dogs respond well to training, they do need firm and consistent **discipline**. For example, if a Cairn barks at a larger dog or other people, its owner should say "No!" until the dog understands that barking is not allowed.

Cairns often chase squirrels. This can be dangerous because a dog can easily run into the middle of a busy street. It's best to keep a Cairn in an enclosed yard or on a leash when outside.

▲ **A woman teaching her dog to sit and stay**

# The Best Little Pals

Though having a Cairn can be a lot of work, owners always say that these pets are the best little pals. It's easy to see why.

For one thing, these dogs are sensitive. They seem to listen and pick up on the feelings of the people around them. They love to spend time with their owners, too. This makes them great companions.

▲ **Cairns enjoy spending time with their owners.**

Cairns are very curious dogs. They always need to know what's going on around them. So in spite of their small size, they make great watchdogs.

20

Cairns also make great family pets because they get along well with older children. They are patient and fun to have around. They enjoy learning tricks such as rolling over and jumping. They also love taking long walks with their owners.

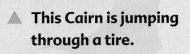

▲ This Cairn is jumping through a tire.

◀ This boy and his Cairn terrier are playing tug-of-war.

# Earthdog

Like their ancestors in Scotland, today's Cairn terriers like to dig for prey. That's why groups such as the Cairn Terrier Club of Denver, in Colorado, hold **Earthdog** events. These events provide a chance for Cairns to do what they were bred to do.

During an Earthdog test, a Cairn terrier must squirm through specially built dirt tunnels searching for prey. This activity is easy for most Cairns. For example, at one recent event in Denver, a young Cairn named Lindsay made her first trip underground. Carefully listening and sniffing, she dug deeper and deeper into the dark tunnel. At last Lindsay let out a yelp. She had found the prey!

▲ A Cairn terrier makes its way out of a tunnel after finding its prey.

▲ A Cairn terrier entering a tunnel

Back in the sunlight aboveground, Lindsay was awarded a ribbon for a job well done. She is now qualified to be an Earthdog!

These five Cairns, shown here with their owners and ribbons, have qualified to be Earthdogs.

In Earthdog events, the prey animal, usually a rat, is kept in a metal cage so it will not be hurt by the Cairn terrier.

# Star Power

Terry's work in *The Wizard of Oz* showed that she had the same hard-working qualities as her Scottish relatives. She spent many long hours learning difficult stunts. For example, she had to jump through windows and over a drawbridge. Smart and brave, Terry mastered these tricks.

▲ **Terry on the set of *The Wizard of Oz* with her costars**

Terry earned $125 a week for her work in *The Wizard of Oz*. That was more money than many of the human actors who appeared in the movie received.

Terry also faced many challenges while working on the movie. In one scene, Terry was put in a closed picnic basket. Active by nature, Terry didn't enjoy being locked up, but she never let that keep her from doing her job. Terry also suffered an injury on the set. One of the actors accidentally stepped on her paw and **sprained** it. However, none of these challenges stopped Terry from finishing the movie and becoming a big star!

▲ **One trick that Terry learned to do in the movie was to open the curtain and reveal the Wizard.**

# A Fan Favorite

Although fans will always remember her as Toto in *The Wizard of Oz*, Terry appeared in 11 other movies, too. Her popularity with audiences opened the studio doors for other Cairns. In the popular 1950s television show *I Love Lucy*, for example, the family dog was a Cairn named Fred. In recent years, Cairns have appeared in more than a dozen different movies. In fact, whenever a script calls for a feisty little dog, people almost expect to see a Cairn.

▲ **Lucille Ball and Fred the Cairn terrier on the set of *I Love Lucy***

The ability to be easily trained and to work hard makes these dogs naturals in show business as well as the perfect family pet. Just as important, their intelligence, sensitivity, and feisty nature grab the hearts of fans watching them on screen as well as the families who adopt them.

Cairns usually live for about 15 years.

▲ **A family enjoying time with their Cairn terrier**

# Cairn Terriers at a Glance

| | Females | Males |
|---|---|---|
| **Weight:** | 13 pounds (5.9 kg) | 14 pounds (6.4 kg) |
| **Height at Withers:** | 9.5 inches (24.1 cm) | 10 inches (25.4 cm) |
| **Coat Hair:** | Short and thick | |
| **Colors:** | Black, gray, red, wheaten, brindled; any color but white | |
| **Country of Origin:** | Scotland | |
| **Life Span:** | 12–16 years | |
| **Personality:** | Sensitive, curious, energetic, intelligent | |

# Best in Show

What makes a great Cairn terrier? Every owner knows that his or her dog is special. Judges in dog shows, however, look very carefully at a Cairn terrier's appearance and behavior. Here are some of the things they look for:

a broad skull

ears that are small and pointed

tail carried high but not curled over

eyes that are set wide apart

a black nose

straight front legs

an outer coat that is course and short; an undercoat that is soft

Behavior: energetic, alert, bold

front feet that are larger than the back feet

# Glossary

**American Kennel Club** (uh-MER-i-kuhn KEN-uhl KLUHB) a national organization that is involved in many activities having to do with dogs, including collecting information about dog breeds, registering purebred dogs, and setting rules for dog shows

**ancestors** (AN-sess-turz) family members who lived a long time ago

**assertive** (uh-SUR-tiv) behaving in a way that is confident and strong

**Best in Show** (BEST IN SHOH) the top-rated dog in a dog show

**bred** (BRED) mated dogs from specific breeds to produce young with certain characteristics

**breeds** (BREEDZ) types of dogs

**coats** (KOHTS) the fur on dogs or other animals

**crofters** (KROF-turz) farmers in Scotland who worked on small areas of land

**discipline** (DISS-uh-plin) to control a person or dog's behavior

**Earthdog** (URTH-dawg) a terrier that has successfully completed a series of trials that test its ability and instincts to hunt animals underground

**feisty** (FYE-stee) very frisky or lively

**groomers** (GROOM-urz) people who wash, comb, and care for animals

**heel** (HEEL) when a dog walks on the left side of a person

**hindquarters** (HINDE-*kwor*-turz) a dog's back legs and lower back

**kennel** (KEN-uhl) a place where dogs are raised or trained; also used as a place for dogs to be looked after while their owners are away

**lineage** (LIN-ee-ij) the line of descent from an ancestor

**litter** (LIT-ur) a group of animals that are born to the same mother at the same time

**prey** (PRAY) animals hunted by other animals

**scrappy** (SKRAP-ee) high-spirited

**sprained** (SPRAYND) injured by twisting or tearing muscles

**standards** (STAN-durdz) the ideal traits and characteristics of the different dog breeds as set by the American Kennel Club and used to judge dogs in dog shows

**undercoat** (UHN-dur-koht) a soft layer of hair covered by a dog's topcoat

**wheaten** (WEET-en) tan or cream in color

**withers** (WITH-urz) the high point of the back of a dog located at the base of the neck

**working dogs** (WURK-ing DAWGZ) dogs that are bred to hunt, herd, or guard

# Bibliography

**The American Kennel Club**. *The Complete Dog Book*. 20th Edition. New York: Ballantine Books (2006).

**Birch, Brenda, and Rich Birch**. *Pet Owner's Guide to the Cairn Terrier.* Lydney: Gloucestershire: Ringpress (2000).

**Lehman, Patricia.** *Cairn Terriers.* Hauppauge, NY: Barron's Educational Series (2009).

**Marvin, J. T.** *The New Complete Cairn Terrier.* New York: Howell Book House (1986).

# Read More

**Goldish, Meish.** *Hollywood Dogs.* New York: Bearport Publishing (2007).

**Mehus-Roe, Kristin.** *Dogs for Kids!* Irvine, CA: Bow Tie Press (2007).

# Learn More Online

To learn more about Cairn terriers, visit
**www.bearportpublishing.com/LittleDogsRockII**

# Index

# About the Author

Duncan Searl is a writer and editor who lives in New York State. He is the author of many books for young readers.